Amazon Dot:

Amazon Dot For Beginners

Everything You Need To Know About Amazon Dot Now

Table of Contents

Introduction

Amazon continuously proves that it is one of the world's leaders when it comes to technological innovations, especially when it comes to what is known as the Smart Home. Over the years, they have come up with many advancements that truly make life easier, the most recognizable of which being Amazon Echo, also known as Alexa.

Alexa then became the catalyst for Amazon, giving birth to one other extremely important item that can truly make a home smart—and it is none other than Amazon Dot.

In this book you will find everything you need to know about Amazon Dot, also nicknamed "Alexa", from how to use it, what are the apps that work with it, and basically how it can make your life better—and so much more! After reading this book, you'd certainly be inclined to buy and use the said device.

Let's begin the journey.

Chapter 1: What Is the Amazon Dot?

Deemed to help you add Alexa in any room of the house, the Amazon Echo Dot, also known as Amazon Dot or Alexa, makes use of the Alexa Voice Service in order to help you do quick searches, learn what you need to know, play music, control devices at home, set alarms, read the news, and do so much more with just the use of your own voice.

How Does It Work?

This form of Alexa is meant to work in any room as it has its own Bluetooth speaker, so it works even when it's not connected to its original external speakers. It is able to stream words and music, thanks to the fact that it makes use of an Advanced Audio Distribution Profile that helps you listen to whatever's streaming on your original Alexa (Amazon Echo) that will then pass through the Amazon Dot. You can also access it through mobile devices, with the help of a great Audio/Video Remote Control Profile.

Another great thing about the Amazon Dot is that dual antenna and dual band Wi-Fi connectivity, so you won't have a hard time going online, and searching for what you need and want.

Whatever Wi-Fi device or connection you use, you can expect that Alexa would be able to connect to it. It also works with the Alexa App that you can open on your iOS or Android devices, and even on the web, so you can make the necessary adjustments whenever and wherever you want!

You should also know that the Amazon Dot weighs 250 grams, and includes a 9W Power Adaptor, a 4 ft audio cable, a quick start guide, and a USB charging cable in the package.

No matter where you are in the house, you can be sure that Alexa will be able to hear you, and therefore, help you, as well. And, you can expect that the quality of service that it gives you will continue to be better as it is meant to keep improving over time.

Different Wake Words, Different Dots

As aforementioned, Amazon Dot can be used in any room of the house, which also means that you can have more than one of it. While its original wake word is simply "Alexa", you can now customize wake words for your different dots. This is a good way of avoiding confusion, and being able to control the device by yourself alone, and so you know that it actually recognizes your voice.

The Alexa App

It's also easy to control the Dot, and it's truly manageable, too, because now, the Alexa App is available for iOS, Android, and even the web. By making use of the said app, you can easily choose the services you want Alexa to be connected to—from music streaming devices, to being able to use the Kindle, ordering pizza for yourself or your friends, setting alarms, and just making sure that there'd be a seamless, one-of-a-kind connection at home.

Aesthetically Pleasing

And, compared to the Echo, the Amazon Dot looks sleeker, and easier to put in any room—helping you make sure that the aesthetics of your home won't suffer, especially if you're using a modern-themed one. It also easily connects to the speakers you have at home so set-up won't be a problem for you.

Setting Up the Dot

In order to use Amazon Dot, of course, it's just imperative that you learn how to set it up first.

To do this, you first have to download the Alexa App on your phone. You can find this on *http://dot.amazon.com/* and make sure that you are using the following platforms:

1. iOS tablets or phones in iOS 7.0 (Apple)

2. Android 4.0 and above (Android/Google)

3. Fire 2.0 and above (Fire tablets/phones)

Then, go ahead and plug the device to an outlet and prepare the remote control by inserting the batteries that came along with it. Once the remote is turned on, it will automatically pair itself with the device. If the remote does not pair, do this: Go to the Dot App in your mobile device then go to *Settings > Amazon Dot > Pair Remote/Forget Remote*. Wait for the devices to pair. If it is unsuccessful, you need to contact Amazon support.

If it is successfully paired, it is time to give your device a name. To do this, go back to your app *Settings* and select *Your Amazon Dot*. Delete this and type the name you want your device to be called. Tap on *Save Changes*. This name has no impact on the wake word of the device, which is still *Alexa* or *Amazon*. The purpose of the name is to simply personalize the device. You may have more than one Amazon Dot in your home and this lets you know which one has been paired to which device or not.

It's also important that you connect the device to the Wi-Fi. The Dot was designed to work only in dual band Wi-Fi. This means that it cannot work on enterprise or corporate type of Wi-Fi connections.

Press and hold the Action button on the device for five seconds. Wait until you see the light turn orange; this is an indication that the device is connecting to your Wi-Fi. Next, go to *Settings > DOT > Update Wi-Fi*. You should see a list of available Wi-Fi connections. Select yours then tap *Connect*.

If you cannot locate your Wi-Fi from the list, scroll down to the bottom and select *Add a Network Rescan*. The device will scan the environment again for available connections. If this still fails, you need to set-up your Amazon Dot device close to the router so it can pick up signals. Signals are usually blocked by walls. Moving your Amazon Dot main unit closer to the router should eliminate issues like this.

Testing the Device

Now, you have to start testing the device. Of course, it all starts with its Wake Word.

The ring on top of the device should turn white—an indication that your Dot is ready and that it is already connected to the

Amazon Cloud or server. The next thing to do is to test if it can hear you. Change the default settings to ensure that it is programmed accordingly. Go the Dot App on your mobile device and select *Settings> [your Dot Name] > Sounds > set Wake Up Sound to Enabled*. Now, test the device. Say the wake word, which is either "Alexa" or "Amazon", and listen closely if you hear a soft beep. It indicates that the device is fully set up.

Amazon Dot, just like other Voice Recognition products, uses a certain mechanism called *on-device keyword spotting* which helps it detect the Wake Word, and also allows it to stream audio to the Cloud, and then there's a certain audio sample that's also sent to the Cloud to help understand what you're trying to say.

However, if there is one family member who is named Alexa, you can change the device's wake up word to Amazon. To do this, go to *Settings > Wake Word > Amazon*.

If you want to make sure that your voice is heard and that the device is connecting you to the Amazon Cloud, go to *Settings > [your Dot name] > Wake Up Sound*. Enable this and the device will produce a beeping sound everytime it wakes up in response to your command. You can also program it to produce a sound once it is done uploading your command to the Amazon Cloud. Do this by enabling *End of Request*.

Amazon's voice recognition program is unparalleled. To date, there were very few complaints logged in Amazon and she sounds almost human, far less robotic than iPhone's SIRI. According to users, the Amazon Dot has less likelihood of misunderstanding your commands than other voice recognition programs. What Amazon does is to record your voice and consistently improve its comprehension and results. And this is something you can do and improve as you go along the voice training program with Alexa.

Chapter 2: Music on the Dot

One of the main things you can do with Alexa is listen to music from your favourite streaming sites. You can either use the audio cable that's included in the package, or make use of Bluetooth speakers to do so.

So, where would you be able to listen to music, then? You actually have a number of choices, and these are:

Amazon Prime. Meant to be the partner of the Amazon Dot, and the Echo, as well, Amazon Prime holds a vast selection of music that one can listen to, or even rent for a certain period of time. It also gives Amazon the knowledge about what type of music their users actually listen to so they could provide them with better selections in the future.

Spotify. Possibly the most popular—with over 100 million active users-- and easy to access streaming site of recent years, Spotify is a Swedish site that allows you to listen to digitally-protected songs and albums from the most popular, and even independent artists around the world. There are times when the site is used by artists to publish new music, especially during Fridays, with the process aptly called "New Music Fridays". With its latest update last August 2016, it was known that there are now over 30 million songs on the said site—proving that you really won't get bored any time you tune in! You can also choose from either a free or premium account, with the difference being premium accounts are ad-free, and that you have the freedom to choose which songs you'd want to play—and which you'd like to skip. Spotify also has a featured called *Spotify Radio* that allows users to listen to handpicked songs depending on genre or mood, such as *Saturday Mornings, Pop, Chillout*, etc.

iHeartRadio. Then, there's also a great internet radio platform named iHeartRadio, where you could feel like you're listening to old-school radio—online! It also serves as what is called a "music recommender system" that gives users an idea of what to listen to next. It has also spawned a music festival, as well as an award-giving body, making it one of the most popular subscription services around. By disliking a song on this platform, you can be sure that it will never be played for you again. There are also certain limitations that you have to follow on the site, such as the fact that you cannot rewind or fast-forward songs, a daily skip rate of only 15 to 16 skips, having to listen to artists that are part of custom stations, and not having the ability to record, but for the most part, it's still a fun and engaging station to use.

Pandora Radio. Then, with the help of Amazon Dot, you can also make use of Pandora Radio, another music recommendation and music streaming service that helps curate playlists based on the genres you have been listening to. You can then choose to give songs the thumbs up, or thumbs down buttons as forms of ratings. It also works with third party applications to provide users with a good selection of songs to choose from.

TuneIn. And of course, there's also TuneIn, which has over 4 million podcasts, programs, and over 100,000 radio stations that you can listen to, with the help of Alexa! It also works not only for Android and Apple, but even for older devices such as the Blackberry, making it easy to use and not intimidating. What's more is that you won't just be able to listen to music, you could also enjoy news, sports, weather, or just about any kind of radio station out there, giving you pure, unadulterated listening pleasure!

How Does It Work?

You have to remember that Amazon Dot was primarily designed to work with Prime, also known as Amazon's very own music streaming service.

This means that you can get access to *iTunes, Pandora, iHeartRadio, TuneIn,* and *Spotify*—just some of the world's most recognized streaming services, which means that you'd really get the best listening experience!

This is a great move for Amazon because their consumers will not feel boxed in a single music platform. There was a time when Apple did this. Almost all their contents—from books to music—are exclusively bought in iTunes. Although this irked many Apple consumers, this did not reduce Apple's fan base because of its constant innovation.

To ensure that you enjoy this feature, you need to consistently update the version of your Amazon Dot app. If you do not do this, your Dot may not work appropriately and failure to update the app can cause very serious problems later on that may force you to completely re-set up the device.

From time to time, Amazon will add extra developments to their products so be in the lookout if there is something new. It is possible that your Dot will not sync so make sure that you are always updated. In addition, you may need new phones that can support upgraded applications. Sometimes, though, you only need to update your existing phone's firmware.

If you are unsure, go to the store of your device's supported platform—Google Play for Android, iTunes for Apple. Look for Amazon Dot. If there is an update button in the store, tap that. If there is none, your device has the most updated version. Your Dot app will also automatically update if there is an existing one, provided you are online. If you set up your phone to ask you first before updating, the Dot app will do just that.

Once you have registered your Dot app, it automatically syncs your Amazon Prime library. This can take some time to complete, especially if you have thousands of songs. If you do not have this set up yet, you'd better be a member so you can enjoy millions of free music. In addition, you can upgrade your account to upload 250, 000 songs to your computer! Even if you don't, you will still get to enjoy a lot of music for free if you are subscribed to Amazon Radio. What's more, if you are registered on Amazon Radio you can tell Alexa to directly purchase the song that you just heard and add it to your library so you can listen to it again and again.

Now, since Alexa is already synced to your Amazon Prime account, you just need to tell her to play a specific song. Say, "Alexa, play [song title].' Alexa will stream your library and play that music right away. If there are two songs of the same title, Alexa will tell you that and you just have to select which artist or album you want her to play.

If the song is not in your library, Alexa will surf Amazon to check if it is available. An alternative to this is using the Dot app from your mobile device. You can open your library from there and pick the specific song you want to play. But this takes out the fun because you want to enjoy the voice recognition intelligence of Alexa. Maybe you should only do this if you are talking to somebody so as not to be disrespectful.

To play music from other libraries, you need to sync them to Dot. Go to *Settings > Music Services* then select your library—iTunes, TuneIN, etc... Once it is full synced, the app will get a list of the songs from your 3rd party music application and relay this to Alexa. You need to say the same command. Only this time, Alexa will not surf your Amazon Prime library. Instead, it will surf your iTunes.

You can tell Alexa to like or dislike a song. You can tell her "thumbs up" or "thumbs down" and she will update your preferences. If you noticed that she is playing the same track once in a while, you can say, "I am tired of this song." What she'll do is to remove this song from your playlist. While playing songs, you can also tell Alexa to stop, pause, or restart. You can also tell her to lop or shuffle or play next song.

Take note that the device can record everything, even a whisper, if it is turned on. You cannot turn this feature off but you can delete recording from the app. This is a security and privacy concern for many people and this is understandable. Amazon made it a point that an Amazon Dot user has the option to delete what has been recorded.

Go to *Manage my Device* page and you can select the recordings you can delete. It is not generally advised to delete everything because it will have a negative impact on how the device recognizes your voice and commands. If you delete everything, you may have to perform voice exercises again.

Here are some of the best music commands you could use:

Alexa, what's playing?
Alexa, Volume 4

Alexa, thumbs up/ Alexa thumbs down (say these when a song from iHeartRadio or Prime Music is playing)

Alexa, stop the music

Alexa, softer

Alexa, shuffle my R & B playlist

Alexa, shuffle my new music

Alexa, resume

Alexa, thumbs up/ Alexa thumbs down (say these when a song from iHeartRadio or Prime Music is playing)

Alexa, I like this song (Also do this when using Prime. This will add a positive rating to the song you have just played)

Alexa, buy this song (for Amazon Music)

Alexa, buy this album (for Amazon Music)

Alexa, shuffle my new music

Alexa, play me the album I just bought

Alexa, play Side to Side

Alexa, shuffle my R & B playlist

Alexa, play the song I just bought

Alexa, play some music by Lorde

Alexa, play jazz from iHeartRadio

Alexa, add this song

Alexa, play a happy song

Alexa, play the song I just bought

Alexa, I like this song (Also do this when using Prime. This will add a positive rating to the song you have just played)

Alexa, buy this song

Alexa, buy this album

Alexa, add this song

Never a Dull Moment at Home

Surely, with the help of Alexa, your house—or even office—would no longer be eerily quiet as you'd be kept company by amazing tunes and sounds, all thanks to the Dot!

Chapter 3: Creating a Smart Home

Another reason why Alexa was created is to help you make your home smarter. You see, smart homes are no longer just the face of the future—they could actually be the face of the present. Life these days is ultimately fast-paced. It is all about being on the go; making sure that you'd get to work on time, have a fantastic social life, and even make sure that things would be so much easier for you.

One way for this to happen is by making use of the Amazon Dot. How could it make your home smarter? Well, Alexa actually works with a couple of apps that are meant to make a home as intelligent as can be, and these are:

Philips Hue. Connecting Alexa with Philips Hue means you'd be able to turn the lights at home on or off, simply with just the sound of your voice. As Philips Hue is a motion sensor in itself, all you have to do is make sure that you tell it which motions to adhere to. You can even ask Alexa to change the colors of lights at home, and even connect the lights to wearables for better control. It's not just for one room of the house, though. You can also control lights at the backyard, the bedroom, the living room, or just about anywhere else at home so you'd feel comfortable. One more way that this can help you is that it allows you to feel better is that it helps you set the mood of the house—and you know that lights can do so much for that.

Insteon. Then, you can also expect the Dot to work with Insteon—an automated app that has been created simply to make things so much easier for you. It could work on tablets, smartphones, or even the computer—and you don't even have to pay anything for it! You can then use it to control the devices you have at home, adjust sensors and switches, and even LED bulbs, thermostat, and control various devices in a side to side manner simply by having it connected to your home internet router.

Samsung SmartThings. Next up is Samsung SmartThings which was truly created for the Internet of Things. What happens here is that you get to make a hub that would help you control client applications and cloud platforms that you are making use of in your daily life. With its help, you can automate even up to a hundred devices or more, providing you with enough sensors that could make your home both smarter and safer!

WEMO. WEMO helps you detect whether if there's something unlawful that's going on at home or so, by helping you gain better control of security cameras and motion sensors, too. You can then record and save footage so you can view them even when you're away from home—right on your mobile devices! You could even stream live footage, too! You could also control bulbs, sockets, cameras, and more!

SONOS. With SONOS, you'd easily be able to control the lights and speakers that you have at home!

Wink. Wink, on the other hand, is something that you could use to manage your automated devices using only one interface—making it easy for you to know what's going on, and if necessary, what needs to be changed and done. What's good about this is that it was created from crowd-sourced ideas, so somehow, it gives you the idea that it's about what people actually want and need. You could then start managing things via a wall-mounted screen, also known as Relay.

Works with Nest. Finally, you also have Works with Nest which will allow you to control the way your devices work—so they just won't follow what's on the manual, but rather, they'd actually follow you. Basically, what you need here is a Nest Thermostat, Nest Cam, or a Nest Protect, and then you can start from there. What's good is that it is secure and private—and you do have full control over it, making you feel like your home is really yours!

How Do You Make These Work?

Making all these work starts with how great you control Alexa. In order to use Alexa the way you want to, you have to make sure that you start training her. You can then follow the Voice Training Exercise below to help Alexa gain skills.

As you progress in the voice training, the device will record your voice multiple times and will help it understand you better. It will record the many ways you say a word and officially recognize that it is you. Alexa will match your speech patterns better and will produce results for you faster and more accurately.

To start voice training, make sure the microphone is turned on by pressing the button on top of the device. Do not use the remote during voice training. Your intent is to record your voice clearly and allow Alexa to process this. Next time you speak to it, even in a muffled voice, Alexa should be able to recognize you. the voice training results will also help the device recognize what you say over the remote control's microphone.

Next, launch your Dot app from your phone, select *Voice Training > Start*.

The system will ask you to read 25 different phrases. Ideally, you should speak from a distance where you will be barking your commands most of the time. You should speak clearly and normally. Do not attempt to toy with the speed or clarity of your speech because the system will record this as a standard reference. Talk to it as you normally would. No need to be self-conscious here. It is a device, not a person who will ridicule you.

If you think you need to repeat a word, tap on Pause in the app and select *Repeat Phrase*. Once done, tap on *Next Phrase* and move on to the next exercises. This exercise can take a while. If you feel tired, you can tap on *Pause* and *End Session* then continue when you feel comfortable.

Even if you skip the exercise, Alexa will still record all the phrases you read and upload it to the Amazon Cloud. You can continue at a later time until you are completely done with the voice training exercise. In addition, the things you say in the voice training exercise will not be record in your dialogue box or panel so it will not be crowded.

Speaking of Skills, you need to keep in mind that these are basically Alexa's voice-driven capabilities. You can actually tweak those skills by enabling or disabling them. Doing so is then called *invocation*. You can do this after activating Alexa, of course.

The thing with skills is that when you make use of specific phrases (i.e., *Turn TV On, Abracadabra Radio, etc.),* you somehow get to communicate with the developer of the original skill. Prime examples would be asking for zip codes, asking Alexa to tell some trivia, or even those Easter Egg commands. As the world progresses, it's important to help the developers work on the app to make them applicable to the world you're living in. Plus, when you help developers enhance Alexa's skills, those skills in turn would contain more information,

Then, Use Bluetooth

Next, you have to be able to control it with the help of the Bluetooth. This is mainly because if you want to experience a pure and clear musical adventure, you should know how to work the Dot through its Bluetooth feature.

With Dot, you do not have to manipulate the recording via your phone. Alexa is equipped with the capability to control playback on your device. All you need to do is to sync her to your device and pick the track you want to play by using voice commands:

1. Play

2. Previous

3. Pause

4. Next

5. Stop

6. Restart

Turn on your phone's Bluetooth and set your phone closely to the Amazon Dot main unit then say, "Alexa, pair." This will prompt Alexa to look for a Bluetooth connection. Once she finds your device she will say, "Ready to pair." Now go to your phone and select Alexa and pair. Once successful, Alexa will tell you, "Connected to Bluetooth." Your mobile handset will also give you the usual Bluetooth confirmation.

Now, you can stream all the songs you want directly from your mobile device. Alexa will play these songs if you use the Dot app or the remote if you do not want to give a voice command. Once you are finished, you can tell Alexa to disconnect. Take note that you cannot send and receive photos and videos using Alexa's Bluetooth technology. Her software does not allow her to do this because she is only a speaker.

Once a Bluetooth device has been paired, Alexa will remember it. You do not have to manually pair it again. As long as your mobile device's Bluetooth is on, you can tell Alexa to pair and she will do it automatically.

And, Don't Forget the Remote

The remote control allows you to give Alexa commands if you are farther than the usual range covered by the device. The remote control has a microphone that allows it to hear you. Once you have given a command, the remote control will relay the signal to the device, then the device will start working on the task you want it to get done.

To tune on the remote, push the button on top of the remote until you hear a beeping sound. Continue holding it down until while you are giving it instructions. The remote control does not have a wake word and does not require one. The remote will also allow you to give orders to Alexa even if the device's microphones are muted. Sometimes, you need to mute the device's microphones if there is too much noise or chatter in the room. The alternative is to use the remote to give it orders.

In Chapter 1, we mentioned that the remote has to be paired with the device. If you lost the remote or if it is damaged, you may order a replacement but you have to pair it again. To do this, go to *Settings > [your Dot name] > Pair Remote/Forgot Remote> Forget*. This command will tell the device to forget the old remote control. Then pair the new remote control.

The remote is also equipped with buttons that allow you to adjust the volumes and, stop, and pause what is blaring through the device. You can use these controls if you do not want to talk to Alexa—times when you are having a conversation with someone and you do not want to be rude.

Review What You Have Told Alexa

You could also review the commands you've been telling Alexa.

All you have to do is access the Alexa app then go to Settings, and choose History. Take note that you'll then see a compilation of commands that you have used categorized into *requests* and *questions*.

To see more detailed entries, all you have to do is tap one of those commands, and you'll be provided with details about it, plus you can also listen to the audio, and you can then provide feedback so that in case Alexa wasn't able to answer it right, you can then tell her how exactly she needs to answer it next time.

Also, you have to take note that history may not really show what you have said verbatim, but you can expect that they will pretty much reflect the commands you have used. It's best that you use the review option, though, because it will help improve Alexa by a mile.

Chapter 4: The Alexa App—and What It Can Do for You

As mentioned earlier, one of the reasons why the Dot is revolutionary is because of the fact that it allows you to make use of the Alexa App, which basically just allows you to do more, and basically, be more as a person. With the Alexa App, you can do a whole lot of things, such as...

Read Whenever and Wherever You Want

One of the things that you can do with the help of the Alexa app is read whenever you want, wherever you want. Well, you can even read however you want, too, as Alexa not only works with Kindle, but also works with Audible—so you can choose whether you'd actually want to read a book, or just listen to it—helping you relax, and catch up with what you have to read in a fast and easy manner!

Shopping on Amazon

Of course, you could also use Alexa to shop for various products on Amazon.

However, you have to make sure that you're only shopping for legitimate products/brands, and products that are also visible on Prime. Your Amazon account addresses and billing information will be the default settings used so you'd easily be able to place orders.

You can also tweak settings by asking for confirmation code, see product and order details, and even turn purchasing off. Orders placed on Amazon Dot are subject to the same rules that are used for Amazon and Amazon Prime Purchases, as well.

The Amazon Dot is programed to add items in your things-to-do-list everytime you give it the right command. Just say, "Alexa, add beer to my to-do list." The device will add this automatically and in addition, the list in your Dot app will also be updated. You can do this in two ways—you tell Alexa verbally to add something in the list or you can go to your app and navigate the to-do-list from the control panel and update it manually.

Alexa can store up to 100 items per list. That is a lot if you really think about it. You can now forget about cluttered papers around your house and forgotten lists. You can tell Alexa to update the list everytime you remember something and also delete some if you want to.

Basically, Alexa supports shopping lists and to-do-lists. You can create your own shopping list so you have it handy when you go to the grocery store. All you need to do is to check it in your smartphone using the Dot app. In fact, you can tell Alexa to buy this instantly from Amazon and deliver it to you for as long as it is available in Amazon.com.

If you are unsure what is in your shopping list, you can ask, "Alexa, what is on my shopping list?" Alexa will enumerate what is on the list and you can tell her to stop or to delete an item. Example: "Delete beer." To tell her to stop, say, "Alexa, stop" or "Alexa, pause."

You also have to remember that there is a long wait list for this device but if you are lucky enough to be even invited, you can toggle something in your account to make the shipping faster. Go to your account settings and go to *Open Orders*. Click this and you will see the tentative date of shipping for your Amazon Dot. Here, select FREE shipping.

If you have already selected a shipping preference before, click that same preference. Then click on *Confirm*. Do not change your original shipping preference to another one because you will be put back to the end of the queue. All you have to do is to click the current shipping preference again, as if to tell the system that you are desperate to have this device now.

Many Amazon subscribers have reported that this trick works but this is not guaranteed. At best, you just have to be patient or buy a second-hand Amazon Dot from online marketplaces.

Manage Your To-Do List

Managing one's to-do list could be such a drag and that's why it's good to know that Alexa could help you manage your to-do list—so you could attend to your appointments and do what you have to do without having a hard time!

Take note that the Amazon Dot is programed to add items in your things-to-do-list every time you give it the right command. Just say, "Alexa, add beer to my to-do list." The device will add this automatically and in addition, the list in your Dot app will also be updated. You can do this in two ways—you tell Alexa verbally to add something in the list or you can go to your app and navigate the to-do-list from the control panel and update it manually.

Alexa can store up to 100 items per list. That is a lot if you really think about it. You can now forget about cluttered papers around your house and forgotten lists. You can tell Alexa to update the list everytime you remember something and also delete some if you want to.

Basically, Alexa supports shopping lists and to-do-lists. You can create your own shopping list so you have it handy when you go to the grocery store. All you need to do is to check it in your smartphone using the Dot app. In fact, you can tell Alexa to buy this instantly from Amazon and deliver it to you for as long as it is available in Amazon.com.

If you are unsure what is in your shopping list, you can ask, "Alexa, what is on my shopping list?" Alexa will enumerate what is on the list and you can tell her to stop or to delete an item. Example: "Delete beer." To tell her to stop, say, "Alexa, stop" or "Alexa, pause."

You could also try the following commands:

1. Alexa, add olive oil to my shopping list.
2. Alexa, create a to-do.
3. Alexa, I need a vet's appointment.
4. Alexa, I need to buy pills.
5. Alexa, I need to go to the country club on Saturday.
6. Alexa, put change tire on my to-do list.

Learning Specifics

Alexa has the capability to give you brand names if you are shopping. You can tell her, "Alexa, what can I buy for my wife?" She will blurt out a list of brand names to choose from. Alexa can also tell you prices at a specific shopping center if you tell her this specifically.

When you want to shop and you are looking for prices within your budget range, you can ask Alexa for some great some deals. The Dot app will display those that are within your budget range. This should help you balance your spending and keep your financial life healthy.

Get Localized or Precise Information

See, what's great about Alexa is that it doesn't give you information that you probably wouldn't use—such as the weather in the other side of the coast, or the nearest restaurant in Nice, France, if you're actually from Los Angeles, California. Anyway, Alexa is still working for US Zones—as of now—so, if you ask Alexa what tomorrow's weather will be immediately after finishing the setup, you might end up disappointed. This is because the Dot needs to correctly get your location before giving out such information.

In order to set this, go back to your settings and enter your zip code on the "Dot device location" option. This will allow you to get the correct news (both local and international), and even pre-recorded shows relative to your area.

Since Dot is configured to use only US zip codes, it cannot read localized information from others.

You may decide to go around this by typing in a US zip code anyway, though the time won't work right. If you use the local time, your setup may also be affected as some countries do not implement daylight saving time (which the Dot is configured to use by default). Either way, you will not be able to access weather, traffic, and news reports that suit your region.

Alarm and Timer

Now, you do not need a separate alarm clock because Alexa can wake you up based on your desired time. Sure enough, you already have an alarm clock in your mobile phone but the speakers of Alexa are better.

You have to command Alexa to wake you up at a specific time by saying, "Alexa, wake me up at 7:30 AM." Alexa will automatically set the alarm. What is good about this is even if you set the device in mute, Alexa will not stop alarming until you tell her to snooze.

Once you tell her, "Alexa, snooze," she will stop but will start blaring again after nine minutes. Alexa will not reset the alarm herself. You need to tell her to set the alarm at the same time again.

The timer works in the same fashion. You can tell Alexa the number of hours or minutes before she alarms. From time to time, she will tell you how much time is left on the timer. You also have to tell her to "pause timer" if this is what you want her to do.

For this, you could also use the following commands:

1. Alexa, cancel the alarm.
2. Alexa, set the alarm for 8:30 a.m.
3. Alexa, set the timer for 10 minutes.
4. Alexa, wake me up at 6 in the morning.
5. Alexa, how much time is left on my timer?
6. Alexa, what time is it?
7. Alexa, when's my alarm set for?
8. Alexa, stop. (this is used for timer alarm)
9. Alexa, snooze.
10. Alexa, what's the date?

Sports and Athletics

Alexa is also one big pop culture geek, and a big sports fan, too! Just make sure you have connected certain apps, such as *Pandora, TuneIn*, or *iHeartRadio,* amongst others, to your Amazon Dot account. Try the commands below and see what Alexa will tell you.

1. Alexa, did the Spurs win?
2. Alexa, I need a Foo Fighters Station from Pandora.
3. Alexa, play Fox Sports on iHeartRadio.
4. Alexa, play Kiss FM on TuneIn.
5. Alexa, play NPR.
6. Alexa, play RadioLab.
7. Alexa, what's the score of the LA Lakers game?

Find the Best Books and Restaurants

If you are looking for a book, you can tell Alexa to search a specific genre—could be comedy, drama, or horror. Once you ask Alexa, she will give you suitable options that you can choose from and she will also give you a summary.

Remember, you can use the 1-Click buying power if you have decided which book you want to buy.

Alexa can give you a list of the best restaurants in your neighborhood. She can also give you the latest deals or promotions as far as restaurants are concerned. Just tell her, "Alexa, give me restaurant deals."

Traffic + Weather Information

To get traffic information, first you need to use the Dot app on your phone. You need to set the starting location and your destination. The app, through Alexa, will suggest a route to you. Alexa will also tell you the expected travel time. Some examples of how to ask for traffic are:

1. Alexa, give me an alternate route?
2. Alexa, what is a good commute route?
3. Alexa, what is the expected travel time?
4. Alexa, what is the traffic situation?

To determine the weather, just tell her to tell you the weather and mention a date. Remember, Alexa will only produce the weather forecast for the ZIP code associated with your Amazon account.

The News

Alexa will also provide you news if you ask her to. There is a service called Flash Briefing in which Alexa provides the hottest news updates from the Internet. You have the flexibility to customize this as per your requirement by going through the app and setting up your preferences. It is up to you if you want to set up you own categories or use the default. You can choose from the following categories:

1. Business

2. Sports

3. Financial

4. Entertainment

Keep in mind that Amazon will provide news information from preselected news sources only and the information you get may have limitations form city to city.

Chapter 5: Alexa's Skills—What They Mean and What They Can Do

When you say skills, you'd probably get to think about the things that someone can do in a great manner, maybe even better than others as these are innate to that individual. Same goes for Alexa: She has skills that you can hone—but only if you'd actually tell her what needs to be done.

Alexa's skills help make life easier for you—and help you realize that life is definitely easier with it around. To help you know what you can do with Alexa, here's a good rundown of that.

The Food Network

You can ask Alexa to help you find the recipe from a show that you just watched on this channel—so you can actually follow what's shown on TV!

Domino's

You could ask Alexa to order you a Pizza from Domino's and have it delivered straight to your doorstep—now, there'd be no more need to call these people on your own as Alexa would do the ordering for you, all thanks to the Alexa App, too!

Capital One

Learn more about your financial standing by asking Alexa to check your account summary.

Evernote

Evernote is like your own online notepad where you could basically just store everything! Now, you can connect Alexa to Evernote and get updates whenever you add something on your to-do list.

Todoist

Todoist is yet another app that reminds you of what you have to do. You could now also get it connected to Alexa.

Keep a spreadsheet of the songs you listen to on Dot

Of course, you can use Alexa to listen to music. But sometimes, you tend to forget what songs you were listening to and end up grasping for answers. In order to prevent that from happening, make sure that you get a spreadsheet of those songs that you have been listening to.

Gmail Shopping List

Get a copy of your shopping list on your email account!

Send email via voice

Yes—no need to use those fingers anymore! If you really are pretty forgetful, and you want someone to also remember you to-do list, make sure that you send them an email, with the help of Alexa!

For example, you told Alexa to add *"Watch How to Get Away with Murder"* to your to-do list, she would then add that to your to-do list, and send it to the person you're trusting with your to-do list, too!

Tweet the Songs You're Listening to on Dot

This basically means that a tweet would be sent every time you listen to a song on Alexa. (i.e., *Listening to Confident by Demi Lovato; Confident by Demi Lovato Now Playing*)

Let Alexa Turn on Television

If you're using Harmony for your TV, you can have it turned on even without using your hands!

Print Your Shopping List

If you need a handy copy of your shopping list—one that you could easily bring everywhere, why not just print it out? Just make sure that your printer is HP, and that you have its ePrint email address.

Find Your Phone with the Help of Alexa

Sometimes, you tend to lose your phone around the house or deep inside your bag, and it feels so frustrating because you'd somehow feel like you would not be able to find it anywhere. Well, when that happens, you can ask Alexa to help you by asking her any sports scores (i.e., *Alexa, what's tonight's NBA Score?)* and what she'll do is make your phone ring while at it! Amazing, huh?

Add Shopping List to Android Wear Notification

If you have an Android Watch, or any other form of Android Wear Product, you can also help remind yourself of your shopping list by sending it to the said product!

Post the Song You're Currently Listening to on Dot to Facebook

Maybe, you should start with a fun recipe, and this one is one of those. What you can expect from this is that whenever you listen to a song on Dot, it will automatically be sent as a status update to Facebook. For example, *Listening to I feel the earth move by Mandy Moore from Coverage!*

Queue a Phone Call

You know how speed dials worked back in the day, right? Well, you can get a push notification to remind you that you need to call someone, and Alexa will tell you about it. For example:

I'd like to [call Anne] 4PM today.

To create this skill, choose *Launch Central* as your trigger center.

Emails

Email someone using Gmail, which is known as one of the most professional-looking email services around. Simply connect it to IFTTT and Alexa, and you're set.

Feed My Fish. If you have some fish to take care of, and you need to be reminded that they have to be fed already, you can ask the help of *LittleBits* and Alexa.

LittleBits is basically an open source library of electronic modules that you can use for learning and prototyping. It's like the cloud, but definitely safer, and more powerful.

For this skill, choose *LittleBits* as your trigger. Then, you can expect to see the message shown below:

[feed my fish]

Water a Zone

There's a smart sprinkler controller called Iro, which can help you maintain your watering schedule, especially when you're so busy and you don't have much time for it. What's great about it is that it automatically changes and adjusts based on the season, and on the current state of the weather. This way, you'd only be using the right amount of water to make sure your garden/landscape is in good shape.

Daily Journal

Hey, it's still great not to let the art of journaling go to waste, you know? Sometimes, you may have some ideas in mind that you need to jot down right away, and you'd feel like having no pens or papers around you might be a problem—don't let it. What you can do is tell Alexa your message for it to directly be saved to *Google Drive*.

Heat the House

No, of course it does not mean that you're going to burn the house and all that, but simply put, you could make the house warmer— or colder—depending on the occasion. This happens with the help of *Nest Thermostat*.

The best thing about the said app is that it takes hold of your schedule, and thinks of the best ways to keep your home comfortable for you. So, what happens here is that you could tweak *Nest Thermostat* to make the house warmer for you, especially during the cold season.

Tweet a Message

Of course, there are also days when you're just a little too busy to update your Twitter account. For that, you have Alexa to help you out with!

Add Shopping List to iOS Reminders

What happens here is when you choose *iOS reminders* as your trigger, whatever you tell Alexa to add in your shopping list will also reflect on your *iOS Reminders*. So, basically, you're reminding yourself twice! No reason to be forgetful now!

Log an Issue

You can also post coding or programming problems on *Github*. *Github* is known as a web app where you can create and share codes, and where you can build apps. So, if there's a certain coding issue that you're facing, you could tell the world about it, too.

Blink Lifx Lights

Lifx are bulbs that you can control depending on the occasion. You can choose it as an IFTTT trigger, and use it in the event that your Amazon Timer goes off.

For the skill, just input something that says that when your Amazon timer goes off, the Lifx lights will blink.

Turn on Belkin Insight Switch

It's always good when you get to wake up to the sight of lights in the morning. It kind of makes the activity more natural, and one good way for this to happen is by making use of Belkin Insight Switch.

Of course, you have to choose *Belkin* as your IFTTT trigger. Now, you can expect the lights to switch on during the time you have set as your "wake up time". For example, you'd tell Alexa to wake you up at 6. Automatically, the lights will turn on at that time, too. Wicked, huh?

The Meat Butler

With the help of this app, you'd learn how to prepare steak, and how to prepare various cuts of meat.

Time Your Workouts

You could tell Alexa to time your workouts, for example, 7 minutes, 15 minutes, maybe even 30 minutes, etc. It's a good way of making sure that you'd get to follow what's included in your training, and ensure yourself of good health, too!

Order Flowers

Alexa has also partnered up with *1-800-FLOWERS*, definitely the most popular online flower shop in the world. You could then ask Alexa to order flowers and send it to whoever you want to send it to—without any hassle!

Meditate and Be in Peace

Alexa also works with an app called *Mindfulness* that you can ask to give you a meditative process that you can follow for certain parts of the day.

Get a Ride

Alexa can also ask *Lyft* to give you a ride so you can reach your destination in time, and without any hassle, too.

Transportation Help

Aside from Lyft, Alexa can also help you get other kinds of transportation, such as knowing the schedule of the L-Train, asking where your bus is, knowing when the next trip of Boston Transit near your place would be, etc. It's like having your own personal assistant—all in the comforts of your own home! Oh, and it works for *Uber* and *Kayak,* too! You'd definitely never get lost anymore!

Tracking Your Steps

Another device that works with Alexa is *FitBit,* you know, that device that tracks how many steps you've taken in a day to help you know how many calories you're burning. You can ask FitBit about the number of steps you've already taken so you can keep track of your health better!

Know What's Going on

Alexa always keeps you in the loop. She'd let you know what's trending on Twitter, what's the latest topic on *The Daily Show,* who's on the *Late Late Show,* etc. This way, even if you have so much to do, you'd still know what's going on in the world around you!

Garegio

Garegio is a Garage-checking app that helps you know whether you've locked the garage and your vehicles are safe or not.

Learn Cat Facts

If you're an ailurophile, that is, being a cat lover, then you might already have the Cat Facts app with you. Well, Alexa could blurt out facts from the app for you, just to give you your much needed catspiration for the day!

Learn Pick-up Lines

If there's someone you want to impress and you want to sound and look cute, then you can also make use of a Pick-Up Lines app to learn some new catchphrases that you can use for that one special person.

Get Affirmations

And of course, you could also ask Alexa to send a Daily Affirmation your way just to have more positive vibes in your day.

You see, Alexa has so many skills—and you can improve them even more. Learn how in the next chapter.

Chapter 6: Teaching the Dot More Skills

Of course, using Alexa doesn't just mean you're just going to take what's being offered and that you wouldn't be thinking of how it can be improved. If you really want to make Alexa yours, why not try the following tips below?

Help Her Compute

We're not talking about your basic 1+1 -- Alexa can also grasp the concepts of floating decimals, so she can tell you the sum of 3.1416 and 2.24756 in a jiffy.

Allow Her to Research

While Alexa cannot recite the Prime Directive for you yet, she can tell you that it was also the title of a Star Trek movie. She can also access the Internet to give you direct facts and figures. She can even research how many calories that scoop of ice cream has!

Some Sense of Pop Culture

Try asking Alexa to beam you up, or try asking her if she is Skynet, and she will give you hilarious answers. She can respond to a wide variety of pop culture references, as well as a collection of Easter eggs. Keep on experimenting with commands.

Some of these Easter Eggs are as follows:

1. Where in the world in Carmen Sandiego?
2. Where have all the flowers gone?
3. Where do you live?
4. Where do babies come from?
5. Where are you from?
6. Where are my keys? (ask twice)
7. When was (Public Figure) elected/other verb?
8. When is the end of the world?
9. When did (movie) come out?
10. When did (event) happen?
11. When am I going to die?
12. What's in name?
13. What was the Oscar Best Picture in 1996?
14. What was the Lorax?
15. What time is it in (name of city)?
16. What is your quest?
17. What is your favorite color?
18. What is the sound of one hand clapping?

19. What is the meaning of life?

20. What is the loneliest number?

21. What is the distance between (location a) and (location b)?

22. What is the definition of_____?

23. What is the best tablet?

24. What is the airspeed velocity of an unladen swallow?

25. What is love?

26. What does the fox say?

27. What do you think of [Apple/Google/Microsoft]?

28. What color is the dress?

29. What color are your eyes?

30. What are you wearing?

31. What are you going to do today?

32. Warp 10

33. War, what is it good for?

34. Volume 11

35. To be or not to be.

36. These aren't the droids you're looking for.

37. Thank you.

38. Testing 1-2-3

39. Tell me a story.

40. Tea. Earl Grey. Hot.

41. Take me to your leader.

42. Surely you can't be serious.

43. Sing me a song.

44. Simon says Wilford Brimley has diabetes.

45. Show me the money!

46. Set phasers to kill.

47. See you later alligator.

48. Say hello to my little friend!

49. Rosebud.

50. Romeo, Romeo wherefore art thou Romeo?

51. Random Fact.

52. Party time!

53. Party on, Wayne.

54. Open the pod bay doors.

55. One fish, two fish.

56. Never gonna give you up.

57. My name is Inigo Montoya.

58. More cowbell.

59. May the force be with you.

60. Make me a sandwich.

61. Make me [breakfast/dinner].

62. Mac or PC?

63. Live long and prosper.

64. Knock knock.

65. Is there a Santa?

66. Is the cake a lie?

67. Inconceivable.

68. I've seen things you people wouldn't believe.

69. I've fallen and I can't get up.

70. I'm home.

71. I want the truth!

72. I think you're funny.

73. I am your father.

74. I [love/hate] you.

75. How tall are you?

76. How much is that doggie in the window?

77. How much do you weigh?

78. How many pickled peppers did Peter Piper pick?

79. How many licks does it take to get to the center of a tootsie pop?

80. How many calories are in (name of food)?

81. How many angels can dance on the head of a pin?

82. How far is (location) from here?

83. How do you make bread?

84. How do I get rid of a dead body?

85. High five!

86. Good night.

87. Give me a hug.

88. Fire photon torpedoes.

89. Elementary, my dear Watson.

90. Does this unit have a soul?

91. Do you want to play a game?

92. Do you want to play a game?

93. Do you want to fight?

94. Do you want to build a snowman?

95. Do you really want to hurt me?

96. Do you like green eggs and ham?

97. Do you know the way to San Jose?

98. Do you know the muffin man?

99. Do you know Siri?

100.   Do you have any brothers or sisters?

101. Do you have a girlfriend?

102. Do you have a boyfriend?

103. Do you believe in life after love?

104. Do you believe in god?

105. Do you believe in ghosts?

106. Define supercalifragilisticexpialodocious.

107. Count by ten.

108. Can you give me some money? (ask twice)

109. Beam me up.

Calculating Dates

Alexa has not yet learned to check how many days there are before the next Superbowl, but you can ask her the number of days before Christmas arrives. You can even ask her how many days are left until your birthday (any date, as long as you specify it) and Alexa will respond accordingly.

Connect Prime Accounts to Dot

This is actually easy. What you have to do is go to the settings page at www.Dot.amazon.com, then choose Set up Household. Of course, it's imperative that members of your family also have Prime Accounts, too.

Now, your family members would just have to download the Dot App, and voila! He can now access Alexa, too!

Connect with Alexa on Your Computer

Aside from being able to control Alexa from its Android or iOS app, you can also just visit Dot.amazon.com, and you'll be able to access to-do and shopping lists connected to Alexa.

Make Alexa Say What She Just Said Again

Just like when talking with other people, there may be times when you would not easily understand what Alexa has just said. What you can do then is ask Alexa to repeat her answer, and you can do this by saying *"Alexa, can you repeat that?"*. Make sure you say this calmly, because saying "Repeat that" without "Please" or "Can You" just makes Alexa a bit more stubborn, as she wouldn't really repeat it.

Use Another Account to Access Alexa

Another great thing about Alexa is that you can actually control it even by using another Amazon account—as long as you have access to that account, of course. What you can do is ask Alexa which profile you're using. Now, make sure that this other Amazon Account of yours is connected to your original account. Ask Alexa to "switch profiles" (i.e., *Alexa, switch to Mary's Profile*) and you're all set!

Create a Software Update Yourself

Just like all devices, software updates also happen to Alexa. But, the thing is, sometimes it feels like you have to wait for the updates and they come when you really do not want them to be there.

According to most users, software updates happen almost every night for Alexa, but if you don't want to wait for that time, go ahead, push the mute button, and allow Alexa to not do anything for at least 30 minutes. Updates would already happen then.

Make Alexa a Bit Stubborn

Of course, Alexa is named "Alexa". That is her Wake Word, which means that whenever you say "Alexa", she will respond. But, what if you're actually just talking about Alexa with your friends and you really don't want the device to do anything?

Well, you can still make Alexa keep quiet. What you have to do is press the mute button on top of the device. After doing so, a red ring will be highlighted and Alexa would stay quiet until such time that you press the button again. This is important at times when you are just talking with your friends, or are in a meeting.

Deleting Voice Recordings

In order to delete voice recordings on Alexa, just open the Alexa app, check Settings, choose History, look for one of those commands that you have made, tap it, and then hit the Delete button.

However, if you want to delete all of the recordings that are associated with your Alexa account and all connected device, you can do so by visiting amazon.com/mycd. Go *to Settings > Manage Content and Devices,* and then select the applicable products.

Household Aboard

The Amazon Dot is not exclusive to only one person. You can invite other adults to be part of the set-up so they can also enjoy using the device. To set this up, tap *Settings > Household Profiles > Invite.* Make sure that the person you are adding is present while you are setting his up. They need to key in their own PIN and details for Alexa to recognize them.

PIN Warning

Of course, it's also important to keep in mind that in order to confirm purchases (if any), you do need to use a PIN. Make sure though that you don't use your credit card PIN so you won't be susceptible to hacking or phishing. Just think of something else that you can easily remember—but that others won't easily guess.

Mask Alexa using a Remote Control

If you have kids around the house, you can make them believe that a remote control is talking to them—or any other inanimate object, too! Simply put Alexa in another room, and then hold the remote/item and say, "*Alexa, Simon Says (followed by what you want it to repeat)*" and Alexa will repeat what you have just said.

Personalize it

Of course, you can customize Alexa to your liking!

To do this, launch the Dot app, go to *Settings > Device Location* then type the ZIP code where the Dot is located the tap *Save Changes*. This allows the Dot to know where you are and give you updated weather reports in your area everytime you ask. Next, change the metric measurements. Go to Settings then change the metrics used for distances, temperature, and measurements.

Chapter 7: Other Commands You Can Use—and Tips to Help Alexa Understand Commands Better!

To totally own the Alexa experience, you need to get an overview of what Alexa can do -- and that is a LOT more than playing music or giving you the news, weather, traffic, and sports updates. But check out this list for starters -- these items should pretty much cover the majority of your daily Dot usage.

Commands Get Better with Voice Training

Alexa is Dot's AI, housed in a cloud server that allows her to grow and learn with each interaction. As her new master, however, you will be the one to show her the ropes -- starting with understanding your speech.

The voice training session will accustom Alexa to your speaking patterns. You will be asked to speak 25 preset phrases. Before beginning, make sure that the Mic Off button has not been activated, and that you are in a location where you would normally be when you start regularly using the Dot. Also, **do not use the remote** when voice training as this can change the results.

To start the session, simply select "Voice Training" from the left panel of your Dot app. If you made a mistake in speaking the phrase, simply hit Pause and the "Repeat Phrase" option. If you need to end the training for some reason, hit "End session" instead (also under Pause). When you finish, click on "Go to Home Page".

Some of the Best Commands You Can Use

Ask Alexa to tell a joke

Just say *"Alexa, tell me a joke."*

Play Rock, Paper, Scissors—and other games!

Alexa, roll a die. (She'll say that she has rolled the die and will give you a number between 1 and 6)

Alexa, heads or tails. (She'll then say that she flipped a coin, and will tell you whether she got head or tail!)

Alexa, roll an N-sided die. (She'll say that she has rolled a N-sided die and give you a number between 1 to N)

Alexa, play Rock, Paper, Scissors. (Alexa will answer with *"Alright, Let's play. 3, 2, 1, Rock/Paper/Scissors"*. She can also play *Rock, Paper, Scissors, Lizard, and Spock— just* like that game in *Big Bang Theory!*)

Alexa, random number between x and y/Alexa, random number between 1 and 15, etc. (Alexa will then give you a random number between x and y)

Alexa, random number (Alexa will give you a random number)

Let Alexa read Wikipedia Entries

Just say *"Alexa, Wikipedia_____"*. For example:

Alexa, Wikipedia Jane by Design

Alexa, Wikipedia the Moon Landing

Alexa, Wikipedia The Matrix

Bluetooth Requests

You can also stream audio from your smartphone through Alexa, but you have to make sure that you have paired the devices. Now, once you have the two connected, you can immediately connect the device (whether smartphone or tablet) to Alexa. Make sure the device is in range, though, and then go and try the following commands:

Alexa, connect my tablet/phone.

Alexa, disconnect my tablet/phone.

Alexa, pair Bluetooth.

One thing you have to keep in mind, though, is that when you ask Alexa to play a specific song or playlist, mobile playback will be paused and disconnected, and you'd only be able to play music from your Amazon Music Library. Just say *Alexa Connect* for you to be able to stream from your mobile device again.

Funny Conversations

Have some fun conversations with Alexa by uttering some of the phrases below:

Alexa, may I kiss you?
Alexa, roll a die
Alexa, random number, please
Alexa, random number between x and y
Alexa, what are the laws of robotics?
Alexa, can you give me some money? (say this twice)
Alexa, sudo (say anything you want)

How much is that doggie in the window?

How much do you weigh?

How many pickled peppers did Peter Piper pick?

How many licks does it take to get to the center of a tootsie pop?

How many calories are in (name of food)?

How many angels can dance on the head of a pin?

How far is (location) from here?

How do you make bread?

How do I get rid of a dead body?

High five!

Good night.

Give me a hug.

Fire photon torpedoes.

Elementary, my dear Watson.

Does this unit have a soul?

Do you want to play a game?

Do you want to play a game?

Do you want to fight?

Do you want to build a snowman?

Do you really want to hurt me?

Do you like green eggs and ham?

Do you know the way to San Jose?

Do you know the muffin man?

Do you know Siri?

Do you have any brothers or sisters?

Do you have a girlfriend?

Do you have a boyfriend?

Do you believe in life after love?

Do you believe in god?

Do you believe in ghosts?

Define supercalifragilisticexpialodocious.

Count by ten.

Can you give me some money? (ask twice)

Beam me up.

Are you sky net?

Are you lying?

Are you in love?

Time Commands

These should make you feel more efficient and productive! These include:

Alexa, what's the date?

Alexa, what time is it?

Alexa, set the timer for 10 minutes

Alexa, set the alarm for 7:30 AM

Alexa, wake me up at 6 AM

Alexa, cancel the alarm.

Alexa, when's my alarm set for?

Alexa, snooze.

Alexa, stop.

Flash Briefing

Flash Briefing is basically Amazon Dot's way of bringing you the latest news, by means of sending you articles, and also with the help of weather updates. You can always customize this on your Amazon Dot account. To let Alexa bring you the latest news, say the following:

Alexa, what's in the news?

Alexa, what's in my Flash Briefing?

Alexa, pause.

Alexa, stop.

Alexa, next article, please.

Autocast and Voicecast + Household Profiles.

If you happen to have a Fire Tablet, you can let it work in sync with Amazon Dot, too.

First, you have to check Settings, followed by Amazon Dot, and then turn *Voicecast* and *Autocast* on. You can do this not only on your device, but also for the device of a friend, or someone at home—but you have to connect that device with Alexa, too. You can do that by going to your account on the Amazon Dot Website.

Then, try the following commands:

Alexa, which profile is this?

Alexa, switch accounts.

Alexa, show this on Adam's Fire.

Alexa, send that file to my tablet.

Alexa, send that to my Fire Tablet.

Additionally, you could also ask Alexa to work on the volume of those programs. For example:

Alexa, help.

Alexa, turn it down

Alexa, louder

Alexa, cancel

Alexa, repeat

Alexa, mute

Alexa, unmute

Alexa, volume five

Fun Facts. Yes, you can also trust Alexa to tell you about mostly anything under the sun. Try asking her the following questions:

Alexa, who wrote Harry Potter?

Alexa, tell me about the Game of Thrones.

Alexa, Simon says jump.

Alexa, tell me a joke

Alexa, why is the sky blue?

Alexa, what's up there?

Alexa, who is the lead singer of The Beatles?

Alexa, what was Britney Spears' first album?

Alexa, how many ounces are there in a cup?

Alexa, what is the capital of Nepal?

Alexa, how far is New York from Antarctica?

Alexa, how old is Barack Obama?

Alexa, when is Thanksgiving this year?

Alexa, Wikipedia: The Sopranos.

Alexa, what is the square root of 64?

Bluetooth Requests. You can also stream audio from your smartphone through Alexa, but you have to make sure that you have paired the devices. Now, once you have the two connected, you can immediately connect the device (whether smartphone or tablet) to Alexa. Make sure the device is in range, though, and then go and try the following commands:

Alexa, connect my tablet/phone.

Alexa, disconnect my tablet/phone.

Alexa, pair Bluetooth.

One thing you have to keep in mind, though, is that when you ask Alexa to play a specific song or playlist, mobile playback will be paused and disconnected, and you'd only be able to play music from your Amazon Music Library. Just say *Alexa Connect* for you to be able to stream from your mobile device again.

Chapter 8: Understanding the Device Even More

Knowing how to use the Amazon Dot is not just about knowing its features or training it into how you want it to be like. It's also about actually learning more about the device—understanding what it looks like, how it works, and what it can do. Aside from the basics that you've learned earlier, here's what else you have to know...

Features

What exactly could you expect from Amazon Dot? How does it look and feel like?

Well, for starters, in comes in the color black, with the dimensions 9.25 x 3.27 inches, with 1 subwoofer that comes in 2.5 inches.

It has 2 inch tweeters, and makes use of Adapter Power, and could be bought for $199!

Homescreen

Take note that the home screen on your Dot app is basically a support system that shows you your most recent interaction with the device. There are home screen cards that you can tap so you can see user-specific controls

You can check out Alexa's homescreen on the Alexa App (more on this later). This means you'll be able to see the following:

1. **Home.** This is the homepage of the device that displays recordings and activities.

2. **Alarm.** This is where you'd set the alarm for the next day, or for other important events and reminders.

3. **Timer.** This shows whether the timer has been turned on or off. This also allows you to put the timer on pause.

4. **List.** This is where you'd see shopping and to-do lists.

5. **Music Provider.** This will show you the device's music library.

From Project D to Dot

During its development stage, it was called Project D, which stands for Doppler that took around four years to finally come into place. The wait's worth it, though, because Alexa is able to do a lot of things. Actually, there are some essential things that you have to know about it—and these are:

It is a Bluetooth speaker

Being a Bluetooth speaker, it means you can stream music from your iPhone6, and you'd be able to experience such a clear quality of sounds, thanks to Alexa's advanced audio design found in a cylindrical chassis inside the microphone.

You see, when you open up Alexa, you'll see that there are speakers that are considered as dual-downward firing that are able to transmit sound all around the room—in 360 degrees!

Apart from that, you'd also be able to see Alexa also has a 2 inch tweeter that provides high and low differences in sound, as well as a 2.5 inch woofer Reflex Port that helps provide clearer, deeper sounds without any form of distortion.

More so, Alexa also comes with music playback controls and a built-in mic that

It Is Said to Be the Predecessor of the "Internet Home"

The Internet Home stems from the belief about the "Internet of Things", which means that one day, every single thing you have at home might be connected to each other for easy functionality.

Since the Amazon Dot will be able to answer your questions and help you out with a lot of things, you can expect that one day, it might be developed into something even better—which would then be able to adhere to the ever-changing world that we're all living in.

It Can Be Used with the Amazon Pen

Recent developments made Amazon release the pen. This is a device that can be paired with Alexa but its main function is to record conversations while you are outside the house. This means you can write ideas literally on paper while the pen is playing what you have previously recorded. Pretty much, this is a recording tool designed as a pen which has a capacity of 4GB of data storage. 4GB is close to storing about 400 hours of talk time. It does not come with the package and has to be purchased separately.

It Always Listens

You see, one of the main things about Alexa is that she can access streaming services—even without a display setting saying that it is now trying to access the said services.

This so happens because Alexa has a seven-microphone array that works like a far-field voice recognition service, which literally means that it's always on—and it's always listening, and it works because of a beam-forming technology that is unique to the Amazon Dot. This also helps Alexa cancel the noise around you so you could just concentrate on the music—or whatever it is that you're trying to stream.

The Search Function Is So Easy to Use

Alexa is basically the cloud streaming service that serves as search function for the Amazon Dot. This is why every time you need to ask it something, you have to say the word "Alexa" first. It's like getting someone's attention: You have to make sure that you know this person, and that you know his name—it's like you're giving Alexa some respect, too, which she really deserves because she'll be able to help you out with a lot of things.

The Various Ring Colors

Another thing you have to understand about the Dot is that various ring colors signify different things about Amazon Dot. Here's what you need to know about them:

Solid Blue

If the color of the ring on top of the device is solid blue, it means that the device is alive—it's awake—and is actually waiting for your commands!

Solid White

If you see solid white, it means that the volume of Amazon Dot is currently being adjusted. For this, you can make use of voice commands, the remote, or through the device itself.

Spinning Blue

This means that the device is either processing or booting up. You'll also notice that the direction of the light will be coming to your direction, and it'll only change direction when you move because it will follow the direction of your voice.

Violet

This color means that the Dot is not able to connect to the Wi-Fi in any way. It's also best that you check the device's signal strength when you get to see this color. You could also try rebooting the modem or the device itself.

Solid Red

Solid Red Light means that the Dot's microphone has been turned off, and that your commands would not be heard—and you also wouldn't get any answers from the device.

No Color

And, if the ring doesn't show any color, it means that even though the device has been turned on, it is still waiting for you to say the wake word. This is because Amazon Dot has been naturally designed to go on "Snooze" mode when it is not being used.

To turn the microphone off, you should push the microphone button on top of the Dot. When you see that it's red, it means you have turned the microphone off, and that it would not respond to your Wake Word. However, it would still respond to your commands as long as you have the Amazon Dot Remote.

The Dot Remote

The Amazon Dot's companion remote control is no less impressive despite its simplicity. It is wireless and voice controlled, and is powered by two AAA batteries. At the very top of its face is a small microphone and right below it is the "Talk Button", activated by pressing and holding it while you speak.

Doing so will result in a brief tone (which can be changed or disabled from the companion Dot App) being played. The beauty of the talk button is that you will no longer need to use the wake word when you give your command, and the Dot will hear you even when the microphone is on mute.

Below these are the playback controls, which also doubles as a trackpad so you can easily control your audio. It features the standard Play/Pause button, as well as previous, next, up, and down.

More Specific Ways to Set Up the Device

The Dot Set Up

Setting up the Dot is really a very straightforward affair. First, you need to make sure there are no obstructions between you and the device -- Amazon suggests placing it in a central location, at least eight inches away from walls, windows, appliances, etc. After this, though, the Dot can be placed literally anywhere, as long as your voice can reach it properly.

1. Plug in your Amazon Dot into any wall socket using the power adapter -- it does not have a backup battery, and will not work when unplugged. The smaller end connects to that little port tucked away at the bottom notch of your device. The genie inside, Alexa, greets you, letting you know that the Dot is ready for setup. She will also hint at the Dot app, which will contain most of the instructions for the process. Wait for the Light Ring to turn blue, and then orange. The orange light is

Amazon greeting you visually.

2. Next, access the Dot app either from your phone or browser -- this will be used to connect the Dot to the WiFi network. Remember that to connect to a network, you should have a dual-band WiFi running at 2.4/5Ghz, and using the 802.11 a/b/g/n standard. The Dot will not be able to connect to peer-to-peer or ad-hoc networks.

3. In the Dot app, you will see the Welcome screen with a button that says "Begin Dot Setup". It also contains different privacy and information retention disclaimers -- be sure to read this thoroughly. If for some reason this did not appear (or if this is not the first time you are using the app to set up an Dot), select the Settings option from the left navigation panel and go to (Your Name)'s Dot. Click on the "Set up a new Dot" option (in the future, you can change your WiFi network by clicking "Update WiFi" instead). From here, proceed to the "Alternate Setup" section below.

4. The next step will be a bit unintuitive, but it is effective -- you will be connecting your mobile device directly to the Dot, as if the latter were a router itself (in effect, you are "capturing" the Dot). While the light on the Dot is orange, hit Continue on the app and go back to access the WiFi settings on your phone. Look for the Amazon network, and wait until connection is established. Afterwards, return to the app -- you should see a "Connected to Dot" screen. Hit Continue.

5. Next, the app will be used to latch the Dot itself on the WiFi network. In the app, select your preferred network, enter the password if needed, and press "Connect". If you know exactly what you are doing, you can set the Subnet Mask, DNS, etc. through "Show Advanced Options".

6. There will be a wait screen that says "Preparing your Dot". After a couple of minutes, the app will prompt you to set up the remote (if you bought it).

The Remote Set Up

First, remember to peel off the protective film on the blaster end of the remote. The remote will not work properly with this on. Next, load two AAA batteries into the remote and press "Forward" (the button to the right of the Play/Pause button). This will automatically pair the remote with the device. Press "Continue", and your set up is completed!

If you are trying to pair the remote after completing the setup (such as when you purchased it at a later time), you will have to take a different route. You will have to go to the app again, select Settings and your Dot's name, and select the "Pair Remote" option. If you happen to see "Forget Remote" there instead, then this means another remote has already been paired (you might be replacing your current one, etc.). Thus, this option will have to be selected before pairing a new one.

After doing so, the device will search for the remote and will attempt to connect with it -- this is usually done in 20 seconds. If your Dot is having any issues searching for the remote, make sure there is no obstruction between the two devices. Hold down the "Play/Pause" button for 5 seconds to send a signal to the Dot -- this facilitates pairing if it doesn't happen automatically.

The Alternate Set Up

The process above would be the default for the initial set up of the device and the app -- i.e., if that is the first time the device or the app is being used. If this is not your first Dot, then an alternate setup is required.

1. Access your Dot app once more and select Settings from its left navigation panel. Go to (Your Name)'s Dot, and click the "Set up a new Dot" option.

2. Back to the Dot itself, press and hold the action button for five seconds. The light will turn orange again, and your mobile device will start connecting to the Dot. On the app, a list of available mobile devices will appear -- select your preferred network from this list, enter the password if needed, and hit the "Connect" button. You can always Rescan or Add a Network in case you do not see your Wi-Fi network from this list (such as if it is hidden). Once the Dot successfully connects, then a confirmation message would pop up on your app.

3. If the Dot fails to connect to the network, you can restart the device by unplugging it then plugging it back into the power socket. If this is not the first time that the Dot is being used, then resetting the device to its factory settings (more on this later) may be the solution.

4. On the app, go back to the home screen. From this point onward, you will be able to use your Amazon Dot!

More about the Hardware

The Amazon Alexa is a round speaker. Once you receive the package, check if you have the complete accessories as outlined below.

The Amazon Alexa

Power cord and adapter

Remote-control holder

Remote control device

Quick Start Manual

AAA Batteries for the remote control

The device is made of metal finish—round in shape to help reduce space consumption. It 3.27 inches in diameter. The Amazon Alexa's main hardware is the Texas Instruments DM 3725 ARM Cortex-A8 processor. It also has 256 MB of LPDDR1 RAM and a storage capacity of 4GB. These things ensure that Alexa will perform at optimal capacity at such speeds that will amaze you. This power, however, needs to be supplemented with good Internet speed.

On top of the Alexa is a ring that serves as an indicator of its status. The ring will turn blue if it is turned on and is ready to use. Later on we will discuss the different colors and what they indicate.

It is also equipped with microphones—this is where Alexa draws the command. The microphones should catch your voice for Alexa to process your commands. Overall, there are seven microphones arranged neatly around the device's speaker. Along with the microphones are sensors made of beam technology that allows the device to hear you. These sensors also enable the device to hear you from all angles so you can bark your command from practically anywhere in the house for as long as the device is in range.

Here is a quick look at the specifications of the Amazon Alexa.

Color : Black

Connections : Wi-Fi and Bluetooth

# of Woofers : 1

Woofer Driver Size : 2.5 inches

Power : Adapter

Size : 9.25 inches by 3.27 inches

Price : $199

# of Tweeters : 1

Tweeter Driver Size : 2 inches

The Amazon Pen

Recent developments made Amazon release the pen. This is a device that can be paired with Alexa but its main function is to record conversations while you are outside the house. This means you can write ideas literally on paper while the pen is playing what you have previously recorded. Pretty much, this is a recording tool designed as a pen which has a capacity of 4GB of data storage. 4GB is close to storing about 400 hours of talk time. It does not come with the package and has to be purchased separately.

Chapter 9: Personalizing the Dot

Of course, you can customize Alexa to your liking!

To do this, launch the Dot app, go to *Settings > Device Location* then type the ZIP code where the Dot is located the tap *Save Changes*. This allows the Dot to know where you are and give you updated weather reports in your area everytime you ask. Next, change the metric measurements. Go to Settings then change the metrics used for distances, temperature, and measurements.

Making use of other features and making it work in US Territories, Canada, and Mexico

In order to use other special features of Alexa, you have to make sure that you go to your app and then tap *Settings > Voice Purchasing*. Switch it on and then provide a confirmation code.

This is a code that you have to create like as if you are creating a password. This code will be asked of you every time you tell Alexa to make a purchase. Key in this 4-digit PIN and tap Save Changes.

Using the 1-Click Feature

The 1-Click feature is not a new concept. This has been with Amazon for years. If you are making regular purchase in Amazon, you know that the 1-Click feature is enabled when you provided your shipping address and billing information to Amazon. This allows you to click BUY online without ahv9ing to enter these details again. If you set this up on Dot, Alexa will simply get the information logged in your Amazon Account to complete the purchase.

Home Device Connection

As the ultimate home companion, you can connect your light bulbs and tell her to switch them on or off. The number of devices that you can connect is pretty limited as of now because very few appliance manufacturers have made appliances that can be synced to Alexa.

And besides, Alexa is currently programmed only to work on light bulbs and switches. Right now, this technology from Amazon is partnered only with Belkin and Philips products. In the future, Amazon will reveal other devices that you can connect to Alexa such as your thermostat and air conditioning system. This technology will happen; we just need to be patient.

To connect these devices, you need to go to the manufacturer's website and download the app. You can also check your phone's store if it is available there. Set it up and sync it with Alexa. Next, connect the actual device via Wi-Fi in the same Wi-Fi where your Alexa is connected to.

Once this is done, tell Alexa: "Alexa, discover my devices." You can also do this through the app by going to *Settings > Connected Home Devices > Add New Device*. Once Alexa has found your device, she will say, "Discovery is complete. In total, you have [number] devices reachable." Once the syncing is successful, you should also see the device on the app. Now you can tell her to turn on or off the lights!

Saving in a Different Manner

Remember that the Dot does not have an SD card slot, you will have to add your downloaded music from your computer to the cloud -- specifically, the Amazon Music library. This service allows you to import up to 250 tracks for free, and can be accessed as soon as you sign up for an Amazon account online (in case you cannot find it, it is under the "Your Account" dropdown on the upper right). If you are a Prime member, you will be able to stream playlists, stations, and even millions of free music.

Also, remember Amazon AutoRip? Anything you order from Amazon's CD catalog also shows up in digital format under your music library. As a plus, your iTunes library can also be imported (though this counts against the 250 music slots you have for free).

If you have audiobooks in your catalog, these can also be accessed through Dot. As a plus, all of these audio features are voice-controlled -- you can pause, play, and back up to the beginning while you are doing the laundry or taking a shower.

If you would like to listen to Pandora or iHeartRadio, you can do this by linking the third-party accounts to the Dot app. On the Settings menu, click on "Music Services" -- this will give you a list of all services currently accessible by the Dot. Some of these services require a link account, which can be accessed by the button next to the preferred music service.

Learning to Control High Fidelity Speakers

Controlling high fidelity speakers with the Dot is amazing. They could give you a fantastic viewing and listening experience. Now, you can make sure that you wouldn't have a hard time trying to set up SONOS each and every time you need to watch or listen to something because it could automatically work to your liking. How? Just check out the instructions below and you'll find out!

1. Take of the rubber seal found on the bottom of Alexa and then remove the screws.

2. Start connecting pieces by working on 2 mid-range/bass ports together with 1 board-to-wire, also known as flexible wire.

3. Next, cut a total of 4 wires, and connect each of those to the RCA Cable. Make sure power and ground wires have already been stripped. To do this, just cut each piece of the wire at least 2 inches from the back (make sure you have 2 blacks and 2 reds), and then go and re-solder the wires together before soldering the rest of the RCA cable. Cut RCA cables at each end and then solder the wires that you have cut with Alexa.

4. Now, it's time to start testing. Make sure you take off the top cover of Alexa and that RCA Cable has been soldered with each of the speakers power wires all the way to the ground. Reconnect those red and black wires that you have skinned earlier to their corresponding flat wires, and then check if Alexa is working by plugging it to an outlet. You'll know it works if it actually lights up, and then plug the soldered RCA Cable to the back plug of Alexa.

5. Connect Ethernet Cable to your phone's SONOS App and ask Alexa what is the product of 54 and 89. She should say something like *54 x 89 is 4086* and you have to hear this across the room. Before doing this, make sure you have set Alexa's settings to Line-in first.

6. Now, it's time to reassemble Alexa—because you really cannot use her skinned like that, right? What you have to do is take it off the wall, and screw everything back into place, get the wires aligned again, and cover Alexa's bottom.

7. Plug Alexa back in, set SONOS to Line-in, and then talk to Alexa—even away from her, and see if you can hear her response resounding throughout the room.

Raspberry Pi Improved Voice Control

Sure, you can let Alexa do a lot of things, and that's a given—but once you tweak it with Raspberry Pi, it'll automatically play you music when it knows that you're on a break, notify you when you have mail, and even read news—even without asking for it!Here's what you have to do:

1. Prepare Amazon Dot, Amazon Dot Controller, Raspberry Pi, 100 Ohm Resistors, and 3v3 Voltage Regulator.

2. Get one of those V+ Pads that you'd see inside Alexa, and then attach a 3v3 Power Supply to it, and then make a space between GND Pads and Raspberry Pi and attach common ground there.

3. On the outer ring of the voice button contacts, go and solder a wire.

4. Now, solder the wire that you have just worked on earlier between ½ voltage divider, and wait for it to reach 1v8.

5. Set GPIO to high, and make use of the commands you learned to input earlier. You can also make use of the following APIs.

Reminders about using Raspberry Pi for Alexa:

1. Take note that upon using Raspberry Pi for Alexa, it also means that you are basically dissembling the power rails, too, so you do have to be careful.

2. Try to place a piece of wax paper underneath the command/microphone contacts. This way, it could serve as a form of adhesive that would protect Alexa's membrane from being dismembered.

3. APIs work mainly because scripting is used to read voice commands on Alexa. RIP GPIO highs and lows are also controlled by the said APIs, and that's why they work not only for commands, but for the nest itself.

4. SMD headers are always in the right angle, and should be soldered onto the test pads to guard controller board and power supply—even if you tweak commands.

5. You can also try soldering wire wrap onto the outer contact itself.

6. You can use 2x AAA batteries to power the test pad, together with 3v3 regulator.

7. And finally, there are tactile switches that are able to connect RPI GPIOs to one another, and then connect them to a 1v8 rail—or voltage divider—as well.

Control Affordable Light Devices

Simply put, SMART LIGHT devices help control the gadgets or appliances that you have at home. With then, you could control lights, water, electronics, and could also be connected to the *IFTTT* (If This then That) account.

However, SMART LIGHT devices aren't really cheap, and sometimes, all one could do is go for knockoffs, instead.

But, Alexa could actually control Affordable Light Devices—you just have to know the right commands to use. Here's what you should know.

Find Connected Devices. Tell Alexa to *Find Connected Devices* and she'd begin searching for SMART LIGHT or SMART LIGHT-like devices. This happens through the broadcast of UPnP channels over UDP. The M-Search Feature would then start looking for the urn: Belkin Device.

Now, what happens is that the SMART LIGHT Device responds with its URL over UDP (address would be http://<ip>:49153/setup.xml). Then, Alexa would request for the description of the device in HTTP over TCP manner (address would be GET/setup.xml), until finally, the device sends its description back.

Find Light. Now, it's time to utter a command. For example, *Find the kitchen light.* Alexa would then send the *Set Binary State* command to the device. What happens here is that HTTP works with SOAP over TCP. In other words: POST/upnp/control/basicevent1.

Say OK. Just say *OK* to let the device return command confirmation and do what you want it to.

Automatically Control Temperature and Lights at Home

One of the best things that you could ask Alexa to do is control lights and temperature at home. But how exactly will you program Alexa do understand various commands about this?

Well, it's all about programming the app. You can do so by opening the Amazon Dot Web App (*Dot.amazon.com*). Here's what you can do to understand it better.

Clone the Repository. When you open the web app (*Dot.amazon.com*), and see the programming prompt, you might see codes onscreen. Now, go and enter your clone code. It would be *Alexa*.

Tweak Settings. Again, do this in the web app. Sign in with your particulars, and then click *Settings*, followed by *History*. Open *JavaScript Inspector* (do so by clicking *Command + Option + J*). *Paste*, then hit *Enter*.Now, you can set the environmental variables already. Do so for your Nest Information (*NEST_EMAIL NEST_PASS*). Just press *Hue Module* button and wait for incoming connections to enter.

Boot up Sinatra Server. To do so, you have to make sure that you have already installed *Ruby* in the system. Ruby, if you don't know by now, is a programming language that works on the Open Source system, and is meant for productivity—which also means you might have to switch to an Open Source system for your Operating System.

If you want to bundle install, you can do so by choosing *bundle install* in the directory.

Boot the server by typing *ruby app.rb*.

Chapter 10: Troubleshooting the Dot

You have to expect that it's not every day that Alexa would work to the best of its abilities. In these cases, you have to make sure that you get to troubleshoot the problems—and you get them easily solved so you could enjoy using the device again!

Device Not Working Properly

When the orange light on your Dot does not change to white, it means it cannot access the Wi-Fi. To troubleshoot, start by trying to reconnect to the network -- access the Dot app, go to Settings and click on "Update Wi-Fi". Then, follow the alternate set up guide we have mentioned above. Also, make sure that the network itself is not down -- the modem or router may have to be restarted to restore connectivity. Try bringing the Dot closer to the router, or removing any obstructions if possible.

If this does not work, try unplugging the Dot from the power cord for 3 seconds, then plugging it back. While doing this soft reset, check that your Dot has been properly registered in your Amazon account (this can be accessed online, under the "Manage Your Content and Devices" on the "Your Account" dropdown). This section of your Amazon account should correctly register your Dot's name. If all else fails, click "Deregister" under your Dot's name and go through the alternate set up process once again.

It Doesn't Connect to the Cloud

Check the ring color. If the ring is circling blue or solid blue, it is active and connecting to the Amazon Cloud. You can go to *Settings > Dot > Sounds* to make Alexa produce a beeping sound whenever it is streaming to the cloud. Alexa will also produce an *end sound* once it is done searching. If nothing came up, then it means the search failed and you need to do it again.

It Cannot Understand What You Are Trying to Say

Though Amazon has poured its engineering genius into the Dot's voice recognition system, there are times when it cannot understand your command clearly. The first step to resolving this is working on the Voice Training, which will be discussed in the next chapter. When doing the training, make sure that there is no background noise so Alexa can capture the words clearly.

When giving Alexa commands, as well, try minimizing the background noise. Speak clearly and slowly. It is also possible that the question is phrased improperly so Alexa cannot properly understand it.

If Alexa starts playing the wrong song for you, try checking on the app to see if she had understood the command properly. If she did, and the wrong song is still played, this could mean that the song you are asking for does not appear in your library.

If it is a question that Alexa cannot answer appropriately, try prefixing the word "question" before asking. Something like: "Alexa, question, <insert query here>?". Remember that Alexa is still learning, and does not know the answer to everything. Finally, if your question is something that Alexa needs to search the Web for (which is nearly all questions), make sure your Wi-Fi network is properly connected.

It Cannot Connect to the Remote

Troubleshooting an unpaired remote is much like the setup we have discussed earlier. First, make sure that the batteries are still working, then go through the set up process. If your device responds with a spinning purple light, this means that more than one remote is being detected. Hit the Play/Pause button on the one you wish to connect. Remember that only one remote can connect to the Dot at once.

It Cannot Connect to the Bluetooth

Like any other modern speaker worth its name, the Dot can interface with discovered Bluetooth devices. Remember that Bluetooth is a pretty limited connection and the paired devices will have to stay within 30 feet of each other.

When you speak the pair command to the Dot (i.e., "Alexa, pair to my phone"), check your Dot app to see if your phone has been found. Click "Connect" to pair. On the device being connected, make sure that Amazon Dot is selected for pairing.

If you still cannot connect, go to the app's settings and go to the "Bluetooth" option. Clear all currently paired devices by hitting "Remove", and attempt the pairing process once again. In the worst case, try resetting the device again by unplugging it from the power outlet for three seconds.

Resetting Alexa

If the basic troubleshooting steps here do not resolve the concern, you can do a complete factory reset of the Dot. Keep in mind that this will erase all settings, accounts, paired devices, etc. that you already entered -- essentially, it will be as if you have just unboxed the Dot.

To do this, get a paper clip or anything similar and look for the Reset button. This button is hidden deep within an unsuspecting hole in a notch near the power adapter port (at the bottom of the device). Press and hold this button, and the Light Ring will turn orange for a moment, and then blue. Wait for the ring to turn off then back on, and go through the entire setup process again.

Sending Feedback to Amazon

You can provide feedback by going to your app and selecting *Settings> Dialog History > Feedback > Send Email.* You can type your feedback here and send to Amazon.

Chapter 11: Amazon Dot FAQs

Here's a compilation of common questions regarding Alexa—all answered for your convenience!

I'm still confused as to how Amazon Dot can really be used. Can you help me understand more?

Well, what you can keep in mind is that Amazon Dot is made to help make your life easier.

Now, Amazon Dot works with a Cloud Service called *Alexa*. Think of *Siri*. Think of the *Google Voice* command. This is why every time you want it to do something, you'd have to say *"Alexa, what is today's weather?"* or *"Alexa, tell me a joke"*, etc. It makes the device understand that you're requesting for it to help you with something.

How exactly does it recognize the Wake Word?

Amazon Dot, just like other Voice Recognition products, uses a certain mechanism called *on-device keyword spotting* which helps it detect the Wake Word, and also allows it to stream audio to the Cloud, and then there's a certain audio sample that's also sent to the Cloud to help understand what you're trying to say.

Is there a way for me to review what I've been asking Alexa?

Yes. All you have to do is access the Alexa app then go to Settings, and choose History. Take note that you'll then see a compilation of commands that you have used categorized into *requests* and *questions*.

To see more detailed entries, all you have to do is tap one of those commands, and you'll be provided with details about it, plus you can also listen to the audio, and you can then provide feedback so that in case Alexa wasn't able to answer it right, you can then tell her how exactly she needs to answer it next time.

Also, you have to take note that history may not really show what you have said verbatim, but you can expect that they will pretty much reflect the commands you have used. It's best that you use the review option, though, because it will help improve Alexa by a mile.

What are Alexa Skills?

Skills are basically Alexa's voice-driven capabilities. You can actually tweak those skills by enabling or disabling them. Doing so is then called *invocation*. You can do this after activating Alexa, of course.

The thing with skills is that when you make use of specific phrases (i.e., *Turn TV On, Abracadabra Radio*, etc.), you somehow get to communicate with the developer of the original skill. Prime examples would be asking for zip codes, asking Alexa to tell some trivia, or even those Easter Egg commands. As the world progresses, it's important to help the developers work on the app to make them applicable to the world you're living in. Plus, when you help developers enhance Alexa's skills, those skills in turn would contain more information, and they would make life even more manageable!

Can I delete Voice Recordings on Alexa?

Yes, you could. Just open the Alexa app, check Settings, choose History, look for one of those commands that you have made, tap it, and then hit the Delete button.

However, if you want to delete all of the recordings that are associated with your Alexa account and all connected device, you can do so by visiting amazon.com/mycd. Go to Settings > Manage Content and Devices, and then select the applicable products.

Can I turn off the Amazon Dot Microphone?

Of course. You can do this by simply pushing the microphone button on top of the Dot. When you see that it's red, it means you have turned the microphone off, and that it would not respond to your Wake Word. However, it would still respond to your commands as long as you have the Amazon Dot Remote.

Can Amazon Dot also be used for shopping?

Yes. However, you have to make sure that you're only shopping for legitimate products/brands, and products that are also visible on Prime. Your Amazon account addresses and billing information will be the default settings used so you'd easily be able to place orders.

You can also tweak settings by asking for confirmation code, see product and order details, and even turn purchasing off. Orders placed on Amazon Dot are subject to the same rules that are used for Amazon and Amazon Prime Purchases, as well.

How will I make the shipping faster?

There is a long wait list for this device but if you are lucky enough to be even invited, you can toggle something in your account to make the shipping faster. Go to your account settings and go to *Open Orders*. Click this and you will see the tentative date of shipping for your Amazon Alexa. Here, select FREE shipping.

If you have already selected a shipping preference before, click that same preference. Then click on *Confirm*. Do not change your original shipping preference to another one because you will be put back to the end of the queue. All you have to do is to click the current shipping preference again, as if to tell the system that you are desperate to have this device now.

Many Amazon subscribers have reported that this trick works but this is not guaranteed. At best, you just have to be patient or buy a second-hand Amazon Alexa from online marketplaces.

How do I purchase music?

You can buy digital music by telling Alexa to do it. The credit card and billing address associated to your Amazon account will be used. A simple phrase like "Alexa, buy [song title]" will prompt Alexa to make the purchase. If you set up the Voice Purchasing feature, Alexa will ask you for your PIN. Purchasing will not work if you did not activate the Voice Purchasing feature.

What happens if Alexa is waking up?

Once you say the wake word, Alexa will connect to Amazon cloud and stay connected. Every word you say will be uploaded in the Cloud and it is the Amazon Cloud that will process your request and send back the signal to Alexa. The signal that Alexa receives will be transcribed to audio and this is what Alexa will say. All these things happen in split seconds, including the research time and all that.

How do I reset the unit if it is not working?

There are two ways to reset the unit: the soft reset and the hard reset. You can use a paper clip to perform a soft reset and insert it in the little hole found under the device. It is like turning it on and off.

For hard reset, you need to turn it off manually and unplug it. The on/off button is found on top of the device. Let it set for 30 minutes to cool down. If the device is unresponsive even if you use the app, you should also unplug it and wait before plugging it back in. If a hard reset, unplugging the device, does not work, leave it unplugged overnight.

How do I know if Alexa is not connecting to the cloud?

Check the ring color. If the ring is circling blue or solid blue, it is active and connecting to the Amazon Cloud. You can go to *Settings > Alexa > Sounds* to make Alexa produce a beeping sound whenever it is streaming to the cloud. Alexa will also produce an *end sound* once it is done searching. If nothing came up, then it means the search failed and you need to do it again.

Can purchasing be turned off?

Yes. Again, you can tweak that on settings. Just visit the Alexa App, go to Settings, and then choose Voice Purchasing, and turn it off.

Hopefully, these have cleared your mind about what Alexa can and cannot do. Don't forget to make the most out of Amazon Dot!

Conclusion

I hope this book was able to help you to understand what the Amazon Dot is, what it can do, and how you can use it to make life better! The next step is to follow the tips mentioned here, and surely, you'd be able to use Dot to the best of its abilities!

I wish you the best of luck!

To your success,

William Seals